UNDERSTANDING NONPROFIT
FINANCIAL STATEMENTS

BY STEVEN BERGER, CPA

SECOND EDITION

BOARDSOURCE
Building Effective Nonprofit Boards

Formerly the National Center for Nonprofit Boards

Library of Congress Cataloging-in-Publication Data

Berger, Steven H.

Understanding nonprofit financial statements / by Steven Berger.-- 2nd ed.

p. cm.

ISBN 1-58686-031-3 (pbk.)

1. Nonprofit organizations-Finance. 2. Nonprofit organizations-Accounting.
  3. Financial statements. I. Title.

HG4027.65.B47 2003

658.15'12--dc21

2003005127

This publication may not be reproduced without permission. Permission can be obtained by completing a request for permission form located at www.boardsource.org. Revenue from publications sales ensures the capacity of BoardSource to produce resources and provide services to strengthen the governing boards of nonprofit organizations. Copies of this book and all other BoardSource publications can be ordered by calling 800-883-6262. Discounts are available for bulk purchases.

The views in each BoardSource publication are those of its author, and do not represent official positions of BoardSource or its sponsoring organizations.

Nothing contained in this book is to be considered as the rendering of legal or financial advice for specific cases, and readers are responsible for obtaining such advice from their own professional counsel. This book is intended for educational and informational purposes only.

BOARDSOURCE

Building Effective Nonprofit Boards

Formerly the National Center for Nonprofit Boards

BoardSource, formerly the National Center for Nonprofit Boards, is the premier resource for practical information, tools and best practices, training, and leadership development for board members of nonprofit organizations worldwide. Through our highly acclaimed programs and services, BoardSource enables organizations to fulfill their missions by helping build strong and effective nonprofit boards.

BoardSource provides assistance and resources to nonprofit leaders through workshops, training, and our extensive Web site, www.boardsource.org. A team of BoardSource governance consultants works directly with nonprofit leaders to design specialized solutions to meet organizations' needs and assists nongovernmental organizations around the world through partnerships and capacity building. As the world's largest, most comprehensive publisher of materials on nonprofit governance, BoardSource offers a wide selection of books, videotapes, and CDs. BoardSource also hosts the National Leadership Forum, bringing together approximately 800 governance experts, board members, and chief executives of nonprofit organizations from around the world.

Created out of the nonprofit sector's critical need for governance guidance and expertise, BoardSource is a 501(c)(3) nonprofit organization that has provided practical solutions to nonprofit organizations of all sizes in diverse communities. In 2001, BoardSource changed its name from the National Center for Nonprofit Boards to better reflect its mission. Today, BoardSource has more than 15,000 members and has served more than 75,000 nonprofit leaders.

For more information, please visit our Web site at www.boardsource.org, e-mail us at mail@boardsource.org, or call us at 800-883-6262.

Dedication:

To Barb, Sam, Ben, Arlie, and Emmalee: You are always on my mind and in my heart.

Have You Used These BoardSource Resources?

VIDEOS

Meeting the Challenge: An Orientation to Nonprofit Board Service

Speaking of Money: A Guide to Fund-Raising for Nonprofit Board Members

Building a Successful Team: A Guide to Nonprofit Board Development

BOOKS

The Board Chair Handbook

Managing Conflicts of Interest: Practical Guidelines for Nonprofit Boards

Checks and Balances: The Board Member's Guide to Nonprofit Financial Audits

The Board-Savvy CEO: How To Build a Strong, Positive Relationship with Your Board

Presenting: Board Orientation

Presenting: Nonprofit Financials

The Board Meeting Rescue Kit: 20 Ideas for Jumpstarting Your Board Meetings

The Board Building Cycle: Nine Steps to Finding, Recruiting, and Engaging Nonprofit Board Members

The Policy Sampler: A Resource for Nonprofit Boards

To Go Forward, Retreat! The Board Retreat Handbook

Nonprofit Board Answer Book: Practical Guide for Board Members and Chief Executives

Nonprofit Board Answer Book II: Beyond the Basics

The Legal Obligations of Nonprofit Boards

Self-Assessment for Nonprofit Governing Boards

Assessment of the Chief Executive

Fearless Fundraising

The Nonprofit Board's Guide to Bylaws

Creating and Using Investment Policies

Transforming Board Structure: New Possibilities for Committees and Task Forces

THE GOVERNANCE SERIES

1. Ten Basic Responsibilities of Nonprofit Boards

2. Financial Responsibilities of Nonprofit Boards

3. Structures and Practices of Nonprofit Boards

4. Fundraising Responsibilities of Nonprofit Boards

5. Legal Responsibilities of Nonprofit Boards

6. The Nonprofit Board's Role in Setting and Advancing the Mission

7. The Nonprofit Board's Role in Planning and Evaluation

8. How To Help Your Board Govern More and Manage Less

9. Leadership Roles in Nonprofit Governance

For an up-to-date list of publications and information about current prices, membership, and other services, please call BoardSource at 800-883-6262 or visit our Web site at www.boardsource.org.

Contents

List of Boxes

List of Exhibits

Preface

Every board member, whether or not on the finance committee, is advised to read this book. Any specific questions on the accounting aspects, standards, or practices should be immediately directed to the organization's finance officers. Board members should receive complete answers and a full understanding of the issues presented in this book. The board should require total satisfaction with its financial information from its administration; otherwise, it will not be meeting its financial oversight fiduciary responsibility. This is a critical element for the board.

Introduction

Every organization exists to provide value. If it did not, the organization would not attract a clientele to sustain it. This is true whether the organization is considered a for-profit entity or a nonprofit entity. The benefits, which are rendered to the organization's clientele, are called "the value proposition." Some of the most common ways to portray value are through customer satisfaction, employee satisfaction, operational excellence, and financial results.

In each case, the value must be defined and measured, but the raw data are not enough to provide meaning. There must be some relative comparison so that the numbers can be understood in a context that renders them meaningful. Take customer satisfaction, for example. Customer satisfaction information is collected, typically through a survey. After the data have been gathered, it is important to determine what the numerical outcomes signify. Let's say that the customer satisfaction survey question being asked was, "On a scale of 1 to 5 (5 being most satisfied), how satisfied were you with the service you received?" If the accumulated result across 1,000 customers was a raw score of 4.1, you may consider this acceptable. Yet, in a comparison of other companies that performed the same services as your organization, if the 4.1 result placed your company in the 62nd percentile, you might rethink the way you perform your services. The 62nd percentile means that your organization was better than 62 percent of the companies performing similar services, but it also means that 38 percent of similar companies or organizations had more satisfied customers than your organization! Ultimately, this type of customer satisfaction result could cause the organization to lose more and more customers until it eventually ceases to exist.

Thus, it is important to understand the implications of the value propositions we specify. This is true for all of the major areas stated above. This book will concentrate on the value proposition of financial statements and their outcomes. For example, some of the more important financial statement ratios that provide value to the reader include the operating margin percentage, the number of days cash on hand, and the debt service ratio.

This book has been organized to maximize a nonprofit board member's understanding of the most important financial elements within his or her organization. At the conclusion of the book, any board member should have a much greater ability to appraise and evaluate such things as balance sheets and assorted statements of cash flow and activities. Board members will also be better able to communicate with the organization's chief executive about the financial outcomes of the organization. This book will also equally allow members of the board to work more closely with administration to set goals for which the administration is responsible to meet, and for which the board is duty bound to monitor.

1.

The Board's Role in Comparison to the Executive's Role

Before getting into the nitty-gritty of the financial information, it is important to separate the roles of the board and the administration. This is significant because as the legal owners of the nonprofit organization, board members have a very different role compared to the chief executive. The board members must be fully informed of the financial and nonfinancial information that they need in order to perform their critical fiduciary responsibilities. The senior management must be resolute in providing this information.

In both theory and practice, there needs to be a clear distinction between the roles and the goals of these groups. As we look at the financial issues and elements of any organization, recognizing the distinct roles will be crucial to its success so that the board can be fully informed by administration in order to perform its fiduciary duties. Box 1 (see page 2) highlights the key roles played by the board and administration. These elements are true whether or not the Internal Revenue Service considers the organization for-profit or nonprofit.

One of the key distinctions between the board and its administration is the fiduciary responsibility board members hold as the purported owners of the organization. The board is charged with ensuring that the organization is being properly managed, from a service and financial perspective. Board members are required to set policies and make sure that these policies are carried out through the practices of management in a legal manner. Thus, the board requires proper oversight of management. This includes the appropriate and timely review of the financial conditions of the organization through review of its financial statements.

In performing their fiduciary role, it is incumbent upon board members to be knowledgeable and informed about their organization's financial status and underlying trends. This is particularly relevant with respect to helping the administration decide how best to manage and optimize resources, especially in fiscally trying times.

BOX 1
COMPARISON OF KEY BOARD AND MANAGEMENT ROLES

Key Board Roles

- Legal responsibility as the organization's nonprofit owners

- Governance, which includes

    1. Setting the long-term vision (including financial)

    2. Establishing policy

- Monitoring the progress towards achieving the vision (actual outcomes compared to the set goals)

- Hiring/firing the chief executive

Key Senior Management Roles

- Collaborating with the board to set the long-term vision

- Managing to achieve the board's vision

- Acting as a responsible liaison between the board and the operating units of the organization

- Providing information to the board that allows for a comprehensive understanding of whether goals are being met, including financial and nonfinancial goals

HINTS FOR BOARD MEMBERS

Be sure to develop a strategic plan for the organization. This will provide the board with a road map for future services and programs over the upcoming five-year period. In addition, quantify the strategic plan by developing a strategic financial plan. This allows the board to determine whether it can fund its plans.

2.

Different Types of Nonprofit Organizations

American corporations can be designated as for-profit or nonprofit. Both types of corporations are allowed to make money, which can be defined as having revenues in excess of expenses. However, nonprofit corporations have been imbued with certain benefits. A key challenge in understanding financial statements is recognizing the many diverse and unrelated types of businesses falling within the sphere of the "nonprofit" definition. Because there are so many different types of industries that are served by the nonprofit sector, no single financial statement example will appear typical.

Section 501(c) of the Internal Revenue code (IRC) creates the definition of organizations that are generally exempt from income and most other federal, state, and local taxes. It includes, among others, charities, social welfare organizations, and associations. With the proper filing requirements met, benefits of 501(c) status include

- Exemption from federal and state income taxes on any profits (excess of revenues over expenses)

- Exemption from property taxes (in most states)

- Exemption from state and local sales taxes, even if they are to be collected

- The ability to obtain bond debt in order to raise capital where the interest income to the purchaser is generally tax exempt, thus allowing the debt to be issued at lower-than for-profit interest rates

Section 501(c)(3) organizations must be operated exclusively for charitable, religious, educational, scientific, or other social welfare purposes. This status comes with additional restrictions; charities must

- Be free of private inurement and private benefit

- Have no substantial involvement in legislative activity

- Have no participation in political campaigns

Being designated as a 501(c)(3) nonprofit organization confers substantial financial benefits not available to for-profit organizations or other tax-exempt organizations. Namely, the ability to accept donations from individuals or corporations, with the donor receiving a tax deduction at the stepped-up fair market (current) value of the donation.

Thus, almost all charities find it extremely important to maintain the IRC 501(c)(3) status. Still, the IRC definition encompasses and embraces thousands of different kinds of nonprofit organizations throughout the country. Major categories of organizations that are considered private charities are included in Box 2. These nonprofit organizations represent many different types of services, different revenue streams (which may include various unrestricted and restricted donations), and different kinds of expenditure rationale (which may include various gifts, grants, services, and administrative overhead expenses).

Throughout the course of the book, we will be utilizing the financial statements of a fictional nonprofit organization. This is meant to be an amalgamation of the many types of nonprofit organizations that operate throughout the country. While it may not look exactly like an organization that you may be familiar with, all the elements are in place so that they may be translated to your organization.

Box 2

MAJOR CATEGORIES OF 501(C)(3) NONPROFIT ORGANIZATIONS

- Religious organizations

- Educational institutions

- Hospitals and other health care providers

- Libraries and research centers

- Community agencies

- Social service organizations

- Foundations

HINTS FOR BOARD MEMBERS

Where possible, have an analysis prepared that quantifies the financial benefits of the organization's tax-exempt status. This allows the organization's board to understand the financial value of the status. It provides talking points when discussing the organization's community benefits.

3.

Differentiating Between Accounting Functions and Finance Functions

In order to gain a better understanding of the financial statements and their purposes, it is important to recognize the concept of the accounting function and how it contrasts with the finance function. There are five major elements to the accounting function. Box 3 highlights these elements.

BOX 3
ACCOUNTING FUNCTIONS

- Identifying and recording all valid transactions

- Classifying financial transactions on a timely basis

- Identifying the time period in which these transactions occurred (accrual accounting)

- Valuing these financial transactions in an appropriate manner

- Disclosing these transactions in an adequate manner

ACCOUNTING FUNCTIONS

The accounting function is designed to allow any reader of the financial statements to gain an understanding of the financial condition of the organization. Each of the five elements of the accounting function is crucial to the proper presentation of the financial information. The first three elements are basic, yet essential to the development and recording of the financial transactions of the organization. The final two elements, **valuation and disclosure**, set the accounting function apart from a pure bookkeeping task.

Valuation is the most crucial element within the accounting function. As we analyze the statement of financial position (balance sheet), it will be obvious that many of the line items are estimates and not actual financial values. These estimates are recorded in the guise of allowances, accruals, adjustments, and reserves. These numbers are, in effect, "valuated" or given a value based on best judgment. Valuation, defined as assigning monetary worth to these items, is the element that establishes accounting as part art as well as part science.

Disclosure, on the other hand, allows all the required elements to be produced in a relatively uniform manner. This is prescribed through the accounting hierarchy known as generally accepted accounting principles (GAAP). The Financial Accounting Standards Board (FASB), through periodic pronouncements known as statements, enumerates disclosure requirements for nonprofit organizations. The American Institute of Certified Public Accountants (AICPA), through a periodically updated *Nonprofit Audit Guide*, sets down other important GAAP requirements. These two sources provide the guidance needed by the organization's accountants and auditors to develop and produce the most reasonable financial statements available for review.

FINANCE FUNCTIONS

The finance function differs dramatically from the accounting function (see Box 4). The accountant's task is to create the accounting information needed for financial review. The financial analyst's job and function is designed to make sense of all the numbers generated by the accountant. It is a not-so-subtle difference. The analyst must be able to get behind the numbers to ascertain trends and tendencies that may have or had positive or negative impacts on the organization. For example, financial analysts develop ratios from the accounting numbers that provide the reader with enhanced information about the organization. These ratios can then be trended across time and compared to other organizations within its industry (also known as benchmarking). Conclusions can then be drawn on the facts determined from the information. These concepts will be addressed in detail later in the book.

BOX 4
FINANCE FUNCTIONS

- Collect

- Analyze

- Communicate

    1. Accounting information

    2. Statistical information

4.

Elements of Basic Audited Financial Statements

There is a well-recognized and generally accepted set of financial information that represents a complete set of basic financial statements. These statements must be reviewed on a periodic basis by an organization's board in order for it to maintain a required level of financial understanding. The following information has been required for nonprofit organizations since 1995 by Financial Accounting Standards Board Statement Number 117 (FAS 117):

- Statement of Financial Position (Balance Sheet)

- Statement of Activities (Income Statement)

- Statement of Cash Flows

- Statement of Functional Expenses (required for voluntary health and welfare organizations only; useful for all other nonprofit organizations)

- Notes (footnotes)

The statements above are the responsibility of management and are typically created monthly. These monthly statements are presented for the month just ended as well as on a year-to-date basis. At year end, the year-to-date figures are the accumulation of the previous 12 months of transaction activities applied to the balance sheet and income statement. FAS 117 requires that the financial statements focus on the entity as a whole, rather than reporting on separate fund groups.

Regardless of the line item that will be reviewed, a critical factor on all the financial statements is that they be reported at net realizable value. This expresses that every line in the financial statements be reduced to the amount that the organization expects either to receive in or pay out as cash. The reductions to the net realizable value are almost always estimates and are developed utilizing generally accepted accounting principles (GAAP) methodologies. Each reduction method will have a considerable impact on the organization's bottom line and financial position; therefore, these elements must be fully understood by the board members. The most influential reductions, which decrease the value of the asset or the income, will be reviewed throughout this text.

OPINION LETTER

Before we review the actual financial statements, it is important to recognize that a complete audited financial statement will include the auditor's opinion letter. This is produced after the organization's external auditors review the year-end figures and pass judgment on whether the management-prepared financial statements are "presented fairly" in conformance with GAAP and in accordance with generally accepted auditing standards. The opinion letter has a basic structure set down through authoritative pronouncements by the Financial Accounting Standards Board and the American Institute of Certified Public Accountants.

Exhibit 1 illustrates a "clean" or "unqualified" opinion letter. From the board review perspective, it is important to note if the opinion letter has more than three main paragraphs. An opinion letter with three main paragraphs typically represents a "clean" opinion. Other than the auditor's choice to emphasize a specific accounting issue in more detail, a fourth paragraph typically means that the auditor believes that the statements are either not in compliance with the GAAP (qualified and/or adverse opinion) or that the auditor is unable to form an opinion due to incomplete information (disclaimed opinion). Any qualified, disclaimed, or adverse opinion calls into question the organization's financial status. Such opinions must be quickly and appropriately addressed by the board's audit and finance committee as well as the board as a whole.

EXHIBIT 1

Little Four
Certified Public Accountants
123 Elm Street
Anytown, State 55555

732-555-1234
www.littlefour.biz

Board of Directors
ABC Charities, Inc.
987 Oak Road
Anytown, State 55555

We have audited the accompanying statement of financial position of ABC Charities, Inc. (a nonprofit organization) as of December 31, 2002 and 2001, and the related statement of activities, cash flows, and functional expenses for the year then ended. These financial statements are the responsibility of the Charities' management. Our responsibility is to express an opinion on the financial statements based on our audit.

We conducted our audit in accordance with auditing standards generally accepted in the United States of America. Those standards require that we plan and perform the audit to obtain reasonable assurance about whether the financial statements are free of material misstatement. An audit includes examining, on a test basis, evidence supporting the amounts and disclosures in the financial statements. An audit also includes assessing the accounting principles used and significant estimates made by management, as well as evaluating the overall financial statement presentation. We believe that our audit provides a reasonable basis for our opinion.

In our opinion, the accompanying financial statements present fairly, in all material respects, the financial position of ABC Charities, Inc. as of December 31, 2002 and 2001, and the changes in net assets and cash flows for the years then ended in conformity with accounting principles generally accepted in the United States of America.

Little Four, CPAs
March 4, 2003

STATEMENT OF FINANCIAL POSITION (BALANCE SHEET)

The statement of financial position, commonly known as the balance sheet (see Exhibit 2), has traditionally been recognized as the most important of all the financial statements due to the information contained in it. This priority, however, recently changed when the Statement of Activities, commonly known as the income statement, took precedence in many boardrooms. This is an offshoot of the intense stock market activity of the 1990s, when the bottom line on the income statement (earnings per share) of most for-profit organizations was scrutinized on a quarterly basis for clues to profitability. Stock prices were influenced accordingly by this measure.

EXHIBIT 2

ABC Charities, Inc.
Statement of Financial Position (Balance Sheet)
at December 31, 2001 and 2002
(in thousands)

	December 2002	December 2001
ASSETS:		
Current Assets		
Cash	1,200	2,000
Investments — Short Term	6,500	5,400
Total Cash and Cash Equivalents	**7,700**	**7,400**
Gross Accounts Receivable	12,000	12,800
Less: Allowance for Doubtful Accounts	(2,800)	(2,600)
Net Patient Receivables	**9,200**	**10,200**
Unconditional Promises To Pay	5,000	5,000
Inventory	500	400
Prepaid Expenses	400	300
Other Current Assets	**900**	**700**
Total Current Assets	22,800	23,300
Long-Term Investments — Unrestricted	62,300	55,000
Trusteed Investments	10,000	12,200
Deferred Financing Costs	1,300	1,400
Other Non–Current Assets	**73,600**	**68,600**
Property, Plant & Equipment		
Land and Land Improvements	2,000	2,000
Buildings	20,000	18,000
Leasehold Improvements	700	700
Equipment and Fixtures	10,500	9,000
Construction in Progress	1,500	1,000
Total PP&E	34,700	30,700
Less: Accumulated Depreciation	(18,000)	(15,000)
Net PP&E	**16,700**	**15,700**
TOTAL ASSETS	113,100	107,600

According to FAS 117, the balance sheet represents and is arranged by the organization's financial assets, liabilities, and net assets (any accumulated financial returns since it came into existence). A nonprofit balance sheet is designed, through double-entry bookkeeping rules (an accounting technique that records every transaction as both a credit and a debit) to conform to the following equation:

Assets = Liabilities + Net Assets

In its simplified definition

- Assets are things that the organization **owns.**

- Liabilities are things that the organization **owes**.

- Net Assets are differences between the financial items that the organization **owns** and **owes.**

	December 2002	December 2001
LIABILITIES:		
Current Liabilities		
Accounts Payable	6,000	4,500
Current Retirement on L/T Debt	1,500	1,400
Total Current Liabilities	**7,500**	**5,900**
Long-Term Debt	64,800	66,200
Other Long-Term Liabilities	2,000	2,100
Total Long-Term Liabilities	**66,800**	**68,300**
TOTAL LIABILITIES	74,300	74,200
NET ASSETS:		
Unrestricted	32,600	27,900
Temporarily Restricted	4,200	4,200
Permanently Restricted	2,000	1,300
TOTAL NET ASSESTS	**38,800**	**33,400**
TOTAL LIABILITIES AND NET ASSETS	113,100	107,600

Thus, cash and property are assets, accounts payable and bond debt are liabilities, and the difference between the assets and liabilities over the course of the organization's existence are the retained earnings, which are called net assets for nonprofit organizations.

Nonprofit board members should be aware that the largest difference between nonprofit and for-profit balance sheets is in the Net Assets section. This section of a for-profit organization is called *Shareholder* or *Owners Equity*. Thus, in the for-profit world, the balance sheet equation is: **Assets = Liabilities + Owners Equity.**

Within the *Owners Equity* section, the major additional line item that will never appear in the nonprofit Net Assets section is "Paid-In Capital," which is the amount of cash contributed into the company as ownership shares. Nonprofit balance sheets will never contain this line because, according to 501(c)(3) rules, there are no equity owners, thus there never will be any paid-in capital.

In this book, we will bring the balance sheet back to prominence due to the important information it provides about the financial position of the organization. This will be the first statement reviewed by the board, particularly those line items that have the greatest impact on the organization's ability to continue operating. Depending on the specific type of services performed by the nonprofit organization, those lines will be

- Assets
  - Cash
  - Accounts Receivable
  - Promises To Give (Pledges Receivable)
  - Property and Equipment (Fixed Assets)
- Liabilities
  - Accounts Payable and Accrued Liabilities
  - Current Portion of Long-Term Liabilities
  - Long-Term Liabilities (typically tax-exempt bonds)
- Net Assets
  - Unrestricted Net Asset Balances
  - Restricted Net Asset Balances

While the numbers have significance to themselves, as we will see later in this chapter and in Chapter 7, a review of even these lines will become somewhat secondary to the ratios that are developed based upon the outcome of these line items.

CASH

Cash is the first asset line on any balance sheet, and with good reason! Cash is the grease that lubricates the operation of any organization. Without a reasonable cash balance, an operation is more likely to decline, contract, and even cease to exist. Cash is the *most important* financial statement element because it allows the organization to meet its current liabilities (amounts owed for goods and services purchased and payroll obligations) as well as pay back its longer-term liabilities such as tax-exempt bonds. On the balance sheet, cash can be classified as current or long-term.

Current cash is generally expressed as

- Checkbook cash (which is immediately available to pay bills)

- Cash equivalents (which are typically money market accounts, easily convertible to cash within one day)

- Certificates of Deposit (if less than 365 days to maturity)

Noncurrent cash is generally expressed as

- Cash designated for capital replacement and acquisition invested in longer-term assets (such as Treasury instruments)

- Trustees' investments (cash set aside from bond proceeds to be used in capital projects)

Recognizing the levels of short-term and long-term (noncurrent) cash is critical to a board member's understanding of the organization's financial health. Information should be presented on a monthly basis in a trended format (preferably as a graph) to highlight the movement of the organization's cash balances.

ACCOUNTS RECEIVABLE

Most nonprofit organizations are not merely philanthropies and foundations; they may be service organizations. Examples include universities, hospitals, and mental health clinics. Organizations that charge for their services are likely to provide those services before payments are made. The amount of money owed by the client / patient / student for the services rendered are known as accounts receivable. In some nonprofits, the accounts receivable may be the largest current asset. As a note, the other side of the accounting transaction that creates the receivable on the balance sheet (a debit) is service revenues on the income statement (a credit).

> **Debit:** Accounts Receivable (recorded on the balance sheet) $15,000
>
> **Credit:** Service Revenue (e.g., tuition) $15,000
> (recorded on the income statement)
>
> This transaction records the amount of money due from Joe Smith (student).

Managing to minimize this asset of accounts receivable is a major goal of these nonprofit organizations. One of the two best ways to move receivables down to zero is through cash collections (at a rate of 100 percent of the receivable). The second method is through write-downs and write-offs, which represent the reduction of expected cash due to issues such as bad debts and contractual obligations. However, while this second method may keep the receivables low, one of the consequences of write-offs and write-downs is the reduction of revenues on the income statement.

Debit: Cash (balance sheet)	$12,000
Debit: Service Revenue Adjustment — Uncollectible (income statement)	$ 3,000
Credit: Accounts Receivable — Joe Smith (balance sheet)	$15,000

This transaction records all the cash collected from the student. The difference is recorded as a reduction to previously recorded service revenue. It expresses that Joe Smith can pay only $12,000 of his tuition instead of the full $15,000.

The above transaction is considered the direct method of write-off for bad debts (uncollectible accounts). The more common method for recording bad debt expenses and write-offs of customer accounts is through the use of an allowance (or reserve) for doubtful accounts. This additional account creates a monthly estimate of the amount of write-offs that *should be* expected against the current accounts receivable balances, based upon the length of time that the accounts have remained unpaid and their historical trends. Typically then, the difference between this month's allowance for doubtful accounts and last month's allowance for doubtful accounts will become this month's bad debt expense, which is an operating expense on the income statement.

This month's allowance for doubtful accounts	$ 5,000
Last month's allowance for doubtful accounts	$ 4,800
Bad debt expense — this month	$ 200

Nonprofit leaders (board of directors and administrators) need to make the maximization of cash collections and the minimization of receivables and bad debts a priority function for the organization's finance division.

PROMISES TO GIVE (PLEDGES RECEIVABLE)

In many nonprofit organizations, unconditional promises to give (previously known as pledges receivable) may represent a significant component of total assets. This is the case where the organization's primary revenue stream results from contributions. As the contributions are promised (but not yet received), the organization will post contribution revenue to its statement of activities and an unconditional promise to give to the balance sheet.

The "unconditional promises to give" balance sheet line should be reported as a net number, already reflecting any estimated reduction for the amount of promises that will be uncollectible. It is the equivalent to the reserve (or allowances) for doubtful accounts applied against the accounts receivable. The amount of the uncollectible is calculated using historical averages and the amount of time that the pledge has remained unpaid.

As with any receivable, it is critical for the organization to minimize the net amount that remains on this line at any given point in time. Good management mandates that these promises be monitored and managed to ensure the maximum receipt of the promised funds in the least amount of time.

PROPERTY AND EQUIPMENT (FIXED ASSETS)

Many nonprofit organizations, particularly those that provide services, such as universities, hospitals, and health care clinics, have a substantial percentage of their assets tied up in fixed assets. Fixed assets are tangible items that are typically classified as land, land improvements, buildings, building equipment, movable equipment, leasehold improvements, and capitalized leases. Organizations develop their own policy for the classification of fixed assets. For example, many organizations classify a fixed asset as merchandise that has a useful life greater than one year and a minimum purchase price of, let's say, $500. Other organizations may choose to utilize a higher minimum purchase price. Keep in mind that this is an organization's prerogative, and is set by policy. The lower the minimum purchase level, the greater the amount of items considered to be fixed assets, and the larger the plant ledger, and vice versa. Note: The plant ledger is a subsidiary ledger of the general ledger, where all the fixed asset elements for each individual piece of property and equipment are recorded. The key elements are the asset's description, the original cost, the annual depreciation expense, and the accumulated depreciation. Nonprofit organizations in various industries will use different policies for setting up their minimum purchase price. Standard industry practices or the capital intensiveness of the industry will often be the factors in setting up an organization's capital policies.

The plant ledger and the balance sheet reflect the *historical cost* of the purchased fixed asset less the amount of money that has been subtracted for the depreciation expense applied against the asset's historical cost throughout the life of each asset. This is known as the *accumulated depreciation*. On the balance sheet, the gross property and equipment totals less the accumulated depreciation equals the net property and equipment line. This is also commonly referred to as *the net book value*.

ACCOUNTS PAYABLE AND ACCRUED LIABILITIES

This line represents the amount of money known to be owed to trade vendors (accounts payable) or estimated to be owed to vendors and suppliers (accrued expenses) that have provided goods or performed services for the organization.

Accounts payables represent all unpaid invoices that have been recorded while accrued expenses are estimates of the costs for services that have been performed, but for which invoices have not been sent by the vendor. Both major items become liabilities for which cash will need to be paid out in the near future.

As shown in Chapter 3, accruals are one of the five major accounting functions and are used to match the time period for which the organization incurred expenses with its revenues. If the accrual concept was not used, then only cash transactions would be recorded on the accounting books. This could be misleading to the reader (e.g., the board member) as the administration could potentially "game" the books by accelerating revenues and slowing down cash payments. While this may appear to improve the outcomes of the organization's financial health at the time the statements are prepared, in reality, the organization may be teetering. For this reason, and also because it is a generally accepted accounting principle, most nonprofit organizations currently use the accrual method of their accounting. It enhances the reader's understanding of the financial statements.

CURRENT PORTION OF LONG-TERM LIABILITIES

The current principal of outstanding bonds due to be paid by the organization within the next 12 months is referred to as current portion of long-term liabilities. Based on the terms of the bonds and the amortization schedule, these payments may be due and payable quarterly, semiannually, or annually. After the original bond issuance is recorded (see Long-Term Liabilities directly below), the current portion is separated out and reported separately on the balance sheet in the current liabilities section.

Debit: Bonds Payable — Long Term (balance sheet) $ 400,000

Credit: Bonds Payable — Current Portion (balance sheet) $ 400,000

This transaction reclassifies the current portion of the principal on the bonds payable from the long-term section to the current liability section.

LONG-TERM LIABILITIES

In many larger nonprofit organizations, the most common type of long-term liability will be tax-exempt bonds payable. In smaller nonprofit organizations, a very common type of long-term liability will be mortgages or notes payable. In either case, this line generally represents the amount of cash that the organization has received (less discounts and other fees) through the issuance of debt. These proceeds are typically used to finance major expansion and renovation projects that will enhance the image or improve the services of the organization. In the case of a bond offering, the accounting treatment for this type of transaction is

Debit: Cash (balance sheet) $ 9,500,000

Debit: Deferred Financing Costs (balance sheet) $ 500,000

Credit: Bonds Payable (balance sheet) $ 10,000,000

This transaction records the cash received and the liabilities created by the issuance of bonds for expansion purposes.

The deferred financing costs will be amortized (allocated) over the life of the bond, which could range from 10 to 30 years. When the deferred costs are reduced on a monthly basis, they become an income statement expense, thus decreasing the operating and net margins.

Debit: Bond Amortization Cost $ 1,389
(may be combined with depreciation)

Credit: Deferred Financing Costs (balance sheet) $ 1,389

This transaction represents the write-off of the deferred financing costs on the balance sheet on a monthly basis over a 30-year period.

($500,000 divided by 360 monthly periods [30 years x 12 months per year])

Note: Mortgage receipts will have similar balance sheet treatments.

UNRESTRICTED NET ASSET BALANCES

Unrestricted net assets are an accumulation of all the organization's financial returns since it came into existence. They are the equivalent of "retained earnings" on a for-profit balance sheet. The unrestricted net asset balances help board members to determine the underlying value of the organization, because essentially, it is the amount of value left over in the organization that the board has discretion over after the total liabilities are subtracted from the total assets. It is always extremely helpful to monitor the trends of the unrestricted net assets over time. The board should expect to see a continuously rising trend for this balance sheet item.

RESTRICTED NET ASSET BALANCES

FAS 117 requires that restricted net assets on nonprofit balance sheets be made up of two major categories: permanently restricted and temporarily restricted. Both of these categories have restrictive covenants set down by the donor. These restrictions may come in the form of time limits and the specific purpose or use of the principal and/or interest. The paragraphs below highlight the differences between temporarily and permanently restricted net assets.

Temporarily Restricted Net Assets — donor restricted, principal and/or interest will be drawn on for specific purposes set down by the donor; restrictions are usually met with the passage of time or purpose being met. An example of a temporarily restricted net asset is a $1,000,000 donation for the operation of a specific service within a charity. The donor stipulates that the $1,000,000 principal cannot be utilized for the services for the first 20 years. Only the interest may be used in the operation. However, at the end of the 20 years, the donor stipulates that the principal will no longer be restricted. Thus, the $1,000,000 will be classified as a temporarily restricted net asset for those first 20 years, at which point, the administration can reclassify it as unrestricted, if it so chooses.

Permanently Restricted Net Assets — donor restricted, principal and/or interest will be drawn on for specific purposes set down by the donor; restrictions never expire nor can they be removed. An example of a permanently restricted net asset is an endowment donated for the express purpose of funding a university faculty position. The endowment may stipulate that the original principal of the donation can never be reduced but the interest earned on the principal will be used to fund the position.

HINTS FOR BOARD MEMBERS

Become familiar with the key elements of the balance sheet and income statement that are estimates for reductions of financial elements down to net realizable value. Be sure to understand the reduction methodologies and determine that it is in compliance with GAAP. Ensure that this has been done correctly by questioning the organization's external auditor about them.

Exhibit 3

ABC Charities, Inc.
Statement of Activities
For the Year-to-Date Ending December 31, 2001 and 2002
(in thousands)

Twelve Months Ended 12/31/2002

	Unrestricted	Temporarily Restricted
PUBLIC SUPPORT AND REVENUES:		
Net Service Revenues	43,600	10,000
Contributions	9,000	-
Grants	3,400	-
Total Support and Revenue	**56,000**	**10,000**
EXPENSES:		
Program Services	40,600	7,000
Management and General	10,190	3,000
Fundraising	710	-
Total Expenses	**51,500**	**10,000**
Excess of Support and Revenue over Expenses	4,500	0
NON–OPERATING INCOME (EXPENSES):		
Gain/(Loss) on investments	1,200	-
Total Non–Operating Income	**1,200**	**-**
Excess of Support and Total Revenue over Expenses		
(Total margin)	5,700	-
Net Assets, Beginning of Year	59,500	4,200
Change in net unrealized gains and losses on investments	(1,000)	-
Net Assets, End of Year	**64,200**	**4,200**

STATEMENT OF ACTIVITIES
(INCOME STATEMENT)

The statement of activities, also known as the income statement, is a compilation of the revenues (from all sources) and expenses of the organization. In reporting these financial elements, the statement will form a conclusion as to the excess of revenue and support over expenses (also referred to as the operating margin) and the change in net assets (also referred to as the net margin). See Exhibit 3.

The audited financial statement requires that the revenues and expenses be reported and classified as unrestricted, temporarily restricted, and permanently restricted.

Furthermore, GAAP requires that the expenses must be reported on a functional basis, categorized into program services, management, and fundraising expenses. These will be presented in the statement of functional expenses, which will be reviewed later in the chapter. There are several important concepts incorporated in the statement of activities that board members should be aware of.

Permanently Restricted	Total 2002	Total 2001	Percentage Change
-	53,600	50,000	7.20%
700	9,700	9,000	7.78%
-	3,400	3,200	6.25%
700	**66,700**	**62,200**	7.23%
-	47,310	45,800	3.30%
-	13,480	12,000	12.33%
-	710	700	1.43%
0	**61,500**	**58,500**	5.13%
700	5,200	3,700	40.54%
-	1,200	1,000	20.00%
-	**1,200**	**1,000**	20.00%
700	6,400	4,700	36.17%
1,300	65,000	62,300	4.33%
-	(1,000)	(2,000)	-50.00%
2,000	**70,400**	**65,000**	8.31%

GENERAL OPERATING EXPENSES

Service Revenues

There are many nonprofit organizations that provide charge-based services to their clients, patients, and/or students. For those organizations, revenues need to be recorded for the services provided. Depending on the industry that the nonprofit inhabits, the recording (posting) of revenues will be in conformance with GAAP within that industry. For example, colleges will record their revenues based on the general accepted methods within university accounting rules, while hospitals will record their revenue based on the generally accepted methods within the health care industry.

These revenues must be reported on the statement of activities at their net realizable value. Thus, if discounts are provided for various classifications of clients, then the discounts must be applied against all the gross revenue being recorded. This is a major tenet of GAAP. If the discounts are not appropriately applied, the statement of activities will be overstated and thus, misleading to all readers including the board.

Contributions for 501(c)(3) Charitable Organizations

Nonprofit 501(c)(3) organizations are legally permitted to accept contributions from individuals or corporations. This is a great benefit to the organization, as it provides additional sources of revenue to meet its mission. This benefit is available because the tax laws allow the contributors (donors) to deduct the current fair market value of the contributions on their tax returns. FAS 116 mandates the accounting for contributions made and received since 1995. According to this statement

- Contributions are defined as being unconditional, nonreciprocal transfers of assets. This means that a contribution with a donor imposed condition, such as a matching requirement, should not be recognized until the condition has been met and, secondly, the donor should not be receiving anything of value back for a contribution to exist.

- Contributions will be recorded not just when cash is received, but also when pledges are made. This means the receiving organization must record pledges receivable and contribution income prior to receiving the cash.

- Contributions will be recorded immediately as income even though the contribution may have had donor restrictions that have not been met. The FASB concluded that restricted contributions only limit the use of the funds but do not result in liabilities. Therefore, the amounts should be recognized as income currently even though the related expenditures that satisfy the restriction may not be made until a future period.

In many public charities, contributions may make up a major portion of the revenues. It is important for board members to understand the rules governing the recognition of contribution revenue. They should also be sensitive to the reporting of the revenues and the types of information they receive in order to appreciate the donors and types of donations that are being made. FAS 116 says that the organization must describe the programs or activities for which the services were used, the nature and extent of the contributed services received during the period, and the amount recognized as revenue. The organizations should also disclose the fair value of contributed services received but not recognized as revenues, if it is practical to do so.

Grants

Many nonprofit organizations are eligible to receive grants, gifts, and bequests, which is another significant benefit of their 501(c)(3) tax-exempt designation. Grants are typically made to nonprofit organizations by corporations and foundations to help the nonprofits meet their charitable mission. Grants can be restricted or unrestricted and are recorded at their fair market value when received.

Grant revenue can be a major source of funding for the nonprofit. It is often used to augment donations and service revenues allowing the organization to provide the services and support needed by its clients, patients, and/or students. Many nonprofits understand that maximizing their grant-gathering opportunities can lead to greater enhanced revenues.

FUNCTIONAL EXPENSES

As stated earlier, FAS 117 requires that expenses must be reported on a functional basis — categorized into program services, management, and fundraising expenses. While practices vary widely as to how expenses are categorized by functional area from organization to organization in the nonprofit sector, it is important to understand the basic rules. Board members should ensure that their organization is following the generally accepted accounting principles and practices within its own industry by questioning its external auditors and through additional reading. The three major categories prescribed by FAS 117 are

1. **Program Services:** These are the goods and services utilized in the production of activities for the organization's beneficiaries, customers, or members to fulfill the purpose or mission of the organization. In general, the most common expenses include salaries and benefits for staff, supplies, purchased services, and even the depreciation allocated for the buildings and equipment used to service the organization's recipients.

2. **Management and General:** This category includes expenses for general oversight, business management, general recordkeeping, budgeting, finance, and other general and administrative activities. This should be clearly distinguishable from expenses for program services. These can also be categorized as indirect, shared, or overhead type expenses, which are essential to program administration but are difficult to allocate to specific programs. A few examples of overhead expenses include allocated portions of a chief executive's time and square footage for shared space (such as restrooms). It is important for boards to recognize the value of these management and general expenses, as they have very specific impacts on the entire operation when added to program service expenditures.

3. **Fundraising:** This category recognizes expenses for publicizing and conducting fundraising events, and preparing and distributing activities involved in the solicitation of contributions from individuals, foundations, government agencies, and others. It is in the interest of the board to understand the expenses it is incurring in the production of fundraising revenues. This is always a useful breakout for the organization, particularly during its planning and monitoring phases.

NON–OPERATING REVENUES AND EXPENSES

Non–operating revenues and expenses are recorded and reported for financial elements that are outside the bounds of the organization's general mission. The primary item usually reported in this section of the statement of activity is realized investment income or losses. There are very specific accounting rules that are required by the organization in this reporting.

Unrealized investment income or losses are not reported in this section of the statement of activities. Instead, according to FAS 124, unrealized gains or losses are reported as changes in net assets.

CHANGE IN NET ASSETS

As stated in the previous section, unrealized income or losses on investments are reported as a change in net assets. FAS 124 requires the reporting on the statement of activities after the total margin line. See the next to last line on Exhibit 3 (page 18). The unrealized income or losses on investments are the differences between the fair values of all the organization's assets that have potential for investment, at the end of the last accounting period and the current accounting period. The Financial Accounting Standards Board decided that these changes in market values needed to be recorded on the nonprofit organization's balance sheet, but they did not want the bottom lines (margins) of the income statement to fluctuate due to these changes. Thus, they determined that the differences be recorded as changes to net assets.

EXHIBIT 4

ABC Charities, Inc.
Statement of Cash Flows
For the Year-to-Date Ended December 31, 2001 and 2002

	2002	2001
Cash Flows from Operating Activities:		
Increase (decrease) in net assets	6,400	4,700
Change in net unrealized gains and losses		
on investments other than trading securities	(1,000)	(2,000)
Increase (decrease) in cash flows from operating activities:		
Depreciation and Amortization	3,100	2,900
Net Accounts Receivable (increase) decrease	1,000	(700)
Other Current Assets (increase) decrease	(200)	1,400
A/P & Accrued Liabilities (decrease) increase	1,500	200
Other Long-Term Liabilities (decrease) increase	(100)	1,000
Current Portion of Long-Term Debt (decrease)	100	100
Net cash provided by (used in) operating activities	**10,800**	**7,600**
Cash Flows from Investing Activities (increase) decrease:		
Net Investments	(5,100)	0
Other Non–Current Assets	0	(200)
Capital Expenditures — Net	(4,000)	(3,500)
Net cash provided by (used in) investing activities	**(9,100)**	**(3,700)**
Cash Flows from Financing Activities:		
Proceeds from the Issuance of Long-Term Debt	0	0
Payments on Long-Term Debts	(1,400)	(1,300)
Net cash provided by (used in) financing activities	**(1,400)**	**(1,300)**
Net Increase (Decrease) in Cash and Cash Equivalents	300	2,600
Cash and Cash Equivalents, beginning of year	7,400	4,800
Cash and Cash Equivalents, end of year	**7,700**	**7,400**

HINTS FOR BOARD MEMBERS

Whenever possible, have the interim monthly financial statements, particularly the balance sheet and the income statement, presented in the same format as the year-end audited financial statement. If done, no translation will be needed to understand any differences between the final year-end interim and audited statements. Any differences will be truly attributable to audit adjustments.

STATEMENT OF CASH FLOWS

The statement of cash flows (see Exhibit 4 on previous page) reports the sources and uses of the organization's short-term cash and cash equivalents for the period concurrent with the statement of activities (income statement). It is a summary of where the organization's cash came from and how it was used. FAS 117 mandated that this statement be required to complete the reader's understanding of a nonprofit organization's financial condition.

Over the years, the statement of cash flows has been a significantly underrated source of information for board members and administrators that is not available elsewhere. The most important line items to review are net investments, capital expenditures, proceeds from the issuance of long-term debt, and payments on long-term debt.

NET INVESTMENTS

If the organization decided to take any of its short-term cash and invest it in higher yielding, longer-term financial instruments (i.e., bonds), the total net value of the investments would be reported on this line of the statement of cash flows. It is important for board members to review this line in order to determine if this was a contributing factor to a reduction of short-term cash.

CAPITAL EXPENDITURES — NET

This is one of the most important lines on the statement of cash flows. It is the only place on the complete set of financial statements that a reader (such as a board member) can determine the total net amount of cash spent on fixed assets. A board member should look at the amount reported on this line and compare it against the depreciation expense reported above it on the statement. Depreciation is an expense reported on the statement of activities (income statement), but it is a non–cash expense, which is why it is added back on the cash flow statement.

If the net capital expenditures plus payments on long-term debt (see previous page) exceed the reported depreciation expense, then the organization has spent more cash on new fixed assets and old debt principal than it recorded as operating expenses. This will typically translate as net cash outlays for the organization. It is an area that may need to be reviewed by administration and the board if the organization is experiencing cash flow shortages.

PROCEEDS FROM THE ISSUANCE OF LONG-TERM DEBT

When the nonprofit organization decides to borrow money for expansion or renovation purposes, or in order to provide new services, it will generally turn to tax-exempt bonds as its means of debt financing. Tax-exempt financing will have a lower interest rate cost than taxable financing, and since it is available to 501(c)(3) nonprofit organizations, it will always be the preferred option.

The proceeds from the issuance of this new long-term debt will be reported on the cash flow statement. It allows the reader to understand that the reason for the increase in cash is associated with the proceeds from the bond issuance.

PAYMENTS ON LONG-TERM DEBT

Whenever an organization borrows long-term debt money, it has an obligation to pay it back! Nonprofit organizations typically borrow money through bond offerings. In traditional bond offerings, interest paybacks are customarily made every six months while the principal payments are made once a year. While the interest expenses are accounted for within the statement of activities as a cash item, the principal payback will not be recorded as an expense.

EXHIBIT 5

ABC Charities, Inc.
Statement of Functional Expenses
For the Year-to-Date Ended December 31, 2001 and 2002

STAFFING EXPENSES	Mental Health	Substance Abuse	Clinic	Total Program Support
Salaries	8,000	6,000	11,000	25,000
Fringe Benefits	1,680	1,260	2,310	5,250
Contract Services	720	540	990	2,250
Total Salaries and Benefits	**10,400**	**7,800**	**14,300**	**32,500**
NON–STAFFING EXPENSES				
Medical Supplies	1,000	400	1,600	3,000
Office Supplies	400	200	380	980
Other Expenses	800	500	800	2,100
Rent Expense	500	720	1,400	2,620
Legal	-	-	-	-
Accounting	-	-	-	-
Bad Debt Expense	500	200	700	1,400
Depreciation — Buildings and Equipment	600	200	1,600	2,400
Interest & Financing Expenses	600	200	1,800	2,600
Total Non–Staffing Expenses	**4,400**	**2,420**	**8,280**	**15,100**
TOTAL EXPENSES	**14,800**	**10,220**	**22,580**	**47,600**

Therefore, the reduction for the cash payback is viewed most clearly on the statement of cash flows. The organization needs to ensure that it has the cash available to meet its debt obligations, and this includes the principal payments as well as the interest. The best sources for these paybacks would be

- Positive cash flows based on positive net margins and/or

- Utilization of depreciation expenses already factored into the net margin calculation

If the organization accesses long-term debt funding through a traditional mortgage rather than a bond, which has a level debt service payment stream (the total payment is the same each month, but as each month passes, the principal payment increases and the interest expense payment decreases), the previous sources of paybacks would still apply.

STATEMENT OF FUNCTIONAL EXPENSES

As stated earlier, FAS 117 requires voluntary health and welfare nonprofit organizations to report expenses by functional expenses (see Exhibit 5 below). Still, many nonprofit organizations have adopted this report, since it helps the reader gain a better understanding of the organization's financial outcomes.

Management and General	Fund-raising	2002 Total Expenses	2001 Total Expenses	Percentage Change
9,000	400	34,400	33,000	4.24%
1,890	85	7,225	6,930	4.26%
-	-	2,250	2,500	-10.00%
10,890	**485**	**43,875**	**42,430**	3.41%
-	-	3,000	2,820	6.38%
200	50	1,230	1,200	2.50%
500	50	2,650	1,970	34.52%
-	25	2,645	2,500	5.80%
300	-	300	280	7.14%
100	-	100	100	0.00%
-	100	1,500	1,000	50.00%
600	-	3,000	2,900	3.45%
600	-	3,200	3,300	-3.03%
2,300	**225**	**17,625**	**16,070**	9.68%
13,190	**710**	**61,500**	**58,500**	5.13%

The primary functional classifications and their FAS 117 definitions are

- Program services — activities that result in goods and services being distributed to beneficiaries, customers, or members that fulfill the purposes or mission for which the organization exists

- Supporting activities

  - *Management and general:* oversight, business management, general record-keeping, budgeting, financing and related administrative activities, and all management and administration except for direct conduct of program services or fundraising activities

  - *Fundraising:* publicizing and conducting fundraising campaigns; maintaining donor mailing lists; conducting special fundraising events; preparing and distributing fundraising manuals, instructions, and other materials; and conducting other activities involved with soliciting contributions from individuals, foundations, government agencies, and others

  - *Membership development:* soliciting for prospective members and membership dues, membership relations, and similar activities

FAS 117 makes clear that the classification system was designed to "help donors, creditors, and others in assessing an organization's service efforts, including the costs of its services and how it uses resources." It allows all interested readers to determine whether the organization is primarily utilizing its revenue and support dollars to achieve its program missions, rather than using it to support administrative efforts. Many of the various industries that are populated by nonprofits, such as the arts, libraries, and others, have developed benchmarks to show the percentage of expenses that are commonly devoted to programmatic services versus supporting services.

Expense allocations may vary dramatically from organization to organization within the nonprofit sector. For example, time spent by an organization's chief executive may rightfully include time that is programmatic rather than administrative. Similarly, the various natural expenses, such as rent, utilities, insurance, and other items should be divided in a logical manner to provide the most reasonable allocation methodology. But the methodology may vary widely among all the organizations in the industry.

This lack of standard allocation practices makes functional accounting less than reliable as a quality benchmark standard. Unless your organization participates in specific benchmarking services that require defined and consistent allocation methods, industry-wide benchmarks should be used with care. Meanwhile, as long as your organization's internal allocation guidelines are reasonable, justifiable, and consistent, they are likely to be accepted by auditors and donors.

EXHIBIT 6

ABC Charities, Inc.
Notes to Financial Statements
Years Ended December 31, 2002 and 2001

1. SUMMARY OF SIGNIFICANT POLICIES

a. Operations

ABC Charities, Inc. is a not-for-profit health services organization, providing general and mental health and substance abuse services.

The Charities is exempt from federal income taxes under Section 501(c)(3) of the Internal Revenue Code and from Federal Unemployment Compensation tax.

Contributions to the Charities are deductible for income tax purposes within the limitations of the law.

b. Basis of Accounting

The accompanying financial statements have been prepared on the accrual basis of accounting and are presented in accordance with Financial Accounting Standards Board Statements No. 117, Financial Statements of Not-for-Profit Organizations. Under SFAS 117, the Charities is required to report information regarding its financial position and activities according to three classes of net assets: unrestricted net assets, temporarily restricted net assets, and permanently restricted net assets. The Charities had unrestricted and temporarily restricted net assets in 2002 and 2001.

c. Net Assets Accounting

ABC Charities reports grants and gifts as restricted support if they are received with donor stipulations that limit the use of donated assets. When a donor restriction expires, that is, when a stipulated time restriction ends or purpose restriction is accomplished, temporarily restricted net assets are reclassified to unrestricted net assets and reported in the statement of activities as net assets released from restrictions. Grants and donations of fixed assets are recorded as unrestricted support, unless explicit donor stipulations specify how those assets must be used.

d. Property and Equipment

Property and equipment are stated at cost or, if donated, at the approximate fair market value at the date of donation.

Depreciation is computed using the straight-line method over the estimated useful lives of related assets, which range as follows:

Land Improvements	20 – 40 years
Building	20 – 40 years
Leasehold Improvements	10 – 20 years
Equipment and Fixtures	5 – 10 years

(continued on next page)

(continued)

ABC Charities, Inc.
Notes to Financial Statements
Years Ended December 31, 2002 and 2001

e. Fiscal Year
The fiscal year ends on December 31.

f. Allocated Expenses
Expenses by function are directly allocated to programs. Other expenses are accumulated in the management and general cost center and allocated to programs.

g. Patient Fee Revenues
All patient fees earned by the Charities are retained within the organization and used to offset the operating expenses.

2. INVESTMENTS
Investments are carried at market value. Income, dividends, realized and unrealized gains and losses are reflected in the statement of activities. The organization invests cash in excess of daily requirements in short-term money market funds.

3. LEASE COMMITMENTS
At December 31, 2002, the Charities was obligated under rental leases for storefront clinic space in several locations. These leases do not meet the criteria for capitalization and are classified as operating leases with the related expenses charged to operations as incurred.

The following is a schedule by year of future minimum lease payments under operating leases as of December 31, 2002, that have initial or remaining lease terms in excess of one year.

Year Ended December 31	Minimum Lease Payments
2003	$ 500,000
2004	460,000
2005	425,000
2006	360,000
2007	315,000

4. SUBSEQUENT EVENT
On January 14, 2003, the Charities was awarded a $5,000,000 grant to inaugurate a new mental health program within its primary service area. The grant is primarily to be used to build a new facility to consolidate a number of its programs.

FOOTNOTES

Every complete set of financial statements includes footnotes (notes) that provide further information to the knowledgeable reader about the organization's financial policies and procedures. Many footnotes are required by GAAP and, in some cases, the format is prescribed. For example, the first footnote on all financial statements will be a summary of significant accounting policies. It is a multipart discussion of the various accounting policies and practices used by the organization in the creation of their own accounting books and records (see Exhibit 6 on pages 27 – 28).

Additional notes may be used to describe, in detail, investments and investment policies, affiliated company investments, property and equipment, lease commitments, contingent liabilities, long-term debts and leases, related party transactions, pension plans, and any significant subsequent events.

From the board perspective, it is extremely important that the board members have a complete understanding of the notes. They are a great source of information about the organization's financial and accounting treatments. Without this additional information, the board members will be lacking a substantial understanding of their own nonprofit financial statements.

5.

Comparisons of Interim and Audited Financial Statements

FINANCIAL INFORMATION

One of the more compelling financial management issues is how boards review financial information on a monthly basis in comparison to their review of the year-end audited financial statements. In other words, is the financial statement format that the board reviews on a monthly basis substantially the same as the format on the one it receives from its external auditor on an annual basis, or is it different? When the formats differ (as is often the case), problems are created for board members.

The year-end audited financial statement format is reported in conformance with generally accepted accounting principles (GAAP) and in accordance with generally accepted auditing standards (GAAS). The auditors are required to set up their audit report within certain criteria prescribed within their industry by the Financial Accounting Standards Board (FASB) and the American Institute of Certified Public Accountants (AICPA). Any interim financial statements that do not match the year-end financial statements will generally not be in conformance with GAAP.

The board has the right to request, from management, that the interim statement be reported in any manner it likes. There may be a plausible reason for the financial statements reviewed by the board to be different than the year-end GAAP format. Not everyone agrees at all times with all GAAP methodology. Although GAAP is developed by industry professionals and is designed to represent the organization's financial information in the least confusing manner, this may not always be the case.

For example, GAAP stipulates that any bond interest expense be reported as an operating expense of the organization. It further stipulates that interest income earned on short-term and long-term assets, with opportunity to invest, be reported as non–operating revenues. This means that the organization's operating margin will be reduced by the amount of the interest expense, although the net margin will reflect the higher earnings represented by the interest income. This will be the case in nonprofit organizations that provide some types of operating services, where the investment income returns are not considered the primary mission.

EXHIBIT 7

ABC Charities, Inc.
Comparison of Statements of Activities
For the Year-to-Date Ending December 31, 2002
(in thousands)

	Format		
	Audit (GAAP) 2002	Interim #1 2002	Interim #2 2002
PUBLIC SUPPORT AND REVENUE:			
Service Revenues	53,600	53,600	53,600
Contributions	9,700	9,700	9,700
Grants	3,400	3,400	3,400
Investment Income	-	*1,200*	-
Total Support and Revenue	**66,700**	**67,900**	**66,700**
EXPENSES:			
Program Services	47,600	47,600	47,600
Management and General	13,190	13,190	*11,990*
Fundraising	710	710	710
Total Expenses	**61,500**	**61,500**	**60,300**
Excess of Support and Revenue over Expenses (Operating margin)	5,200	6,400	6,400
NON–OPERATING INCOME:			
Gain/(Loss) on investments	1,200	-	-
Total Non–Operating Income	**1,200**	**-**	**-**
Excess of Support and Total Revenue over Expenses (Total margin)	6,400	6,400	6,400
Net Assets, Beginning of Year	65,000	65,000	65,000
Change in net unrealized gains and losses on investments	(1,000)	(1,000)	(1,000)
Net Assets, End of Year	**70,400**	**70,400**	**70,400**

In Exhibit 7 for example, a nonprofit board may request (1) that the interim statement of activities be reported with the interest income shown in the revenues section, or alternatively, (2) that the interest expense be offset against the interest income and the "net" amount be reported as interest income in the non–operating section. This allows the board to isolate the "true" operating margin results with both sides of the interest equation factored out.

It is certainly appropriate for the board to be able to review the interim statement in a manner that enhances understanding. Still, the key concept should be that, if interim statements are presented that do not conform to GAAP, then an additional statement should be prepared and presented each month that does conform to GAAP. In this way, the board will be kept fully informed of its financial interests and will not be "surprised" by the year-end audit treatment.

STATISTICAL INFORMATION

GAAP specifically stipulates the types of information required in an audited financial statement. Most interestingly, it does not require any statistical information be reported in the body of the financial statements or in the footnotes, both of which we have already reviewed.

Statistical information certainly enhances the reader's awareness of a variety of issues that may not be conveyed with only the financial information. For example, a foundation may wish to report the number of grants that it approved during the year. This information is important because the gross number of grants should have some bearing on the amount of grant funds that were approved. The information becomes even more important when it is reported across time and as a ratio.

So, if we look at the information in Box 5 (next page), it provides the reader with certain information that would otherwise have been unavailable, and helps to develop conclusions that otherwise would not have been obtainable. Box 5 allows the reader to observe that, although the nonprofit organization paid out more money in the two years since 2000, the amount of dollars approved per grant has declined each year. There may be readers who need to know this information. Perhaps they are donors, or potential donors, and are interested in the trend of dollars per approved grant. If this is the case, then certainly the board should also be receiving this type of information. And yet, the dollars per approved grant is only available when the statistical information, Number of Grants Approved, is reported.

In the many different nonprofit organizations that exist, a plethora of statistical information is available. The organization's management and board should sit down and determine the statistical information that has the greatest impact on the mission and the operations (critical success factors). The actual information, along with the preset goals, should then be reported on no less than a monthly basis. In fact, the statistical information should be the first page of a monthly board financial and operational report. It is the statistics, and the ratios that are derived, that are most critical in the board's understanding of management's performance.

Box 5

STATISTICAL INFORMATION

	2000	**2001**	**2002**
Grant Dollars Approved	$1,000,000	$1,500,000	$2,000,000
Number of Grants Approved	100	160	250
Average Dollars per Approved Grant	$10,000	$9,375	$8,000

6.

How To Use Financial Information To Perform Legal and Fiduciary Responsibilities

There are a number of ways that management and the board can use financial and statistical information to perform legal and fiduciary responsibilities. Initially, the board members must be aware of the specific legal and fiduciary issues involved in the industries in which their nonprofit organization is involved. Every industry has its legal issues.

There can never be a substitute for exceptional board education. This is a two-sided process. First, the organization must provide formal training sessions in all of the essential elements of the organization, including finance, operations, and legal. Second, the board members must make the time to attend these sessions and ask any questions they need answered in order to enhance their understanding. Both sides must show a commitment to this process. If this does not happen, then both sides will be liable for subpar performance. Neither side wants this to happen.

There are two areas board members should be particularly aware of in using financial information to perform legal and fiduciary responsibilities: the IRS informational form and Guidestar.

IRS FORM 990

An organization is deemed a 501(c) nonprofit because the Internal Revenue Service has recognized it as one. The definition of nonprofit organizations was discussed in Chapter 2. Once the organization is designated as a tax-exempt organization, it is exempt from a number of taxes, including federal income taxes on profits. Still, the board member needs to be aware that, although the organization is tax exempt, it is still required to file an informational form annually. This document is known as Form 990. In addition to providing the federal government with all the information it needs, Form 990 has many other uses, which the board should become familiar with.

There are several major elements of information in Form 990. The organization is required to report its revenues and expenses, its statement of financial position (balance sheet), and a number of additional pieces of mandated information. In particular, the organization must fill out a section describing programs and services provided to fulfill its mission. Although Form 990 provides only 12 lines to complete this task, most nonprofit organizations should supplement these lines with as many attached pages as needed to tell their story. This is a critical area for board review.

The Form 990 also requires information on the compensation paid to the officers, directors, trustees, and chief executive officers, as well as the top five compensated employees not in the previous group. Finally, the top five nonsalaried individuals or companies must also be reported along with the remuneration.

There is also a long series of questions that must be answered by the organization on a number of specific topics. At least one board member, presumably from the finance committee, should review these questions before the form is submitted. This type of oversight can only help the quality of the information being presented to the federal government.

GUIDESTAR

There is good reason to provide the cleanest possible Form 990 to the government. Often referred to incorrectly as a 'tax form,' the Form 990 is considered an informational report. Unlike an individual taxpayer's IRS 1040, which has strict confidentiality requirements for disclosure, the 990 is available for anyone who wants to see it. It may be requested from the nonprofit organization and must be turned over in a short period of time.

Since the late 1990s, Philanthropic Research, Inc., a 501(c)(3) public charity founded in 1994, has produced a Web site called www.Guidestar.org. It has compiled as many nonprofit Form 990s as it can and placed them on the Internet. In early 2003, the site had more than 850,000 IRS-recognized nonprofit organizations' Form 990s. So there is an excellent chance that a specific nonprofit's Form 990 is available to anyone at the click of a mouse.

BOND COVENANTS

If a nonprofit organization has any outstanding bonds on the open market, they are likely subject to bond covenants. These agreements may require the organization to meet certain financial ratios at the time of filing the required quarterly and/or annual financial reports. It is incumbent upon the board to make certain that these covenants are reviewed, ensuring that all pledges have been met. The original bond document details the penalties for noncompliance. The harshest of these penalties allows the bond holders to demand immediate payback of the bond funds. This is certainly not a desired outcome.

Board members should be cognizant of the bond covenants and require management to present the bond covenant analysis quarterly and/or annually. Be sure that the analysis includes trends across time (in graph form). This will help the board members to determine if there has been erosion in any of the metrics.

7.

How To Use Financial Information To Determine Organizational Performance

RATIO ANALYSIS

One of the board's primary duties is to monitor the operational performance of management. The best way to do this is through the proper reporting of information: financial, statistical, and operational. We have already analyzed the development and reporting issues surrounding the formal financial statements. These statements are the basis for the additional information provided through ratio analysis, which will supply the board with the most important elements in determining whether its goals have been met.

Ratio analysis is a method for taking two or more informational elements and obtaining additional information. Financial ratio analysis is the technique used to assess financial condition. There are a number of financial statement ratios that need to be reported at least monthly to allow the board to understand its operational outcomes. Box 6 shows the most common ratios that should be reported to the board on a regular periodic (i.e., monthly) basis. Each nonprofit organization should determine the value of each of these ratios to its operation through a review, analysis, and specific understanding. Where applicable, adopt the ratios that help the board gain a greater understanding of its operational outcomes.

CURRENT RATIO

The current ratio is one of the most common ratios, and is used in all industries to measure liquidity. This ratio measures the number of dollars held in current assets as a percentage of the number of dollars owed in current liabilities. A result of 1.0 means that the organization has exactly enough current assets (assets that are convertible to cash within a short period of time — usually within one year) to pay off all of its current liabilities (liabilities that are payable within a short period of time — usually within one year). Organizations should strive to have results in the 2.0 to 4.0 range. This will express to any reader that the organization is financially solvent, having double to quadruple the financial means, in the near term, to pay off its short-term liabilities.

The current ratio is expressed in the following equation:

$$\frac{\text{Current Assets}}{\text{Current Liabilities}}$$

Thus, $22,800 / $7,500 = 3.04 current ratio

QUICK RATIO

The quick ratio is an adjunct to the current ratio. This ratio, also known as the asset-test ratio, measures the organization's ability to meet short-term obligations from its most liquid, or quick, assets. Quick assets are defined as cash or assets quickly and easily convertible into cash, such as marketable securities and accounts receivable — but not inventory.

The quick ratio is expressed in the following equation:

$$\frac{\text{Cash} + \text{Cash Equivalent} + \text{Accounts Receivable} + \text{Unconditional Promises To Pay}}{\text{Current Liabilities}}$$

Thus, $21,900 / $7,500 = 2.92 quick ratio

DAYS CASH ON HAND

This is perhaps the most important of all the ratios. Days cash on hand measures the number of days of average cash expenses that the organization maintains in either short-term sources or all sources. Like the current ratio, a higher value will always be preferred. Readers will be able to assess the organization's ability to meet its financial obligations based on the outcomes from this ratio.

The two ratios of days cash on hand are expressed in the following equations:

$$\text{Days Cash on Hand (Short-Term Sources)} =$$

$$\frac{\text{Cash} + \text{Short-Term Investments}}{(\text{Total Expenses} - \text{Depreciation}) / 365}$$

Thus, $1,200 + $6,500 / (($61,500 − $3,200) / 365) = 48.2 days cash on hand

$$\text{Days Cash on Hand (All Sources)} =$$

$$\frac{\text{Cash} + \text{Short-Term Investments} + \text{All Long-Term Investments}}{(\text{Total Expenses} - \text{Depreciation}) / 365}$$

Thus, $1,200 + $6,500 + $62,300 + $10,000 / (($61,500 − $3,200) / 365) = 500.8 days cash on hand

It should be noted that cash from short-term or all sources might include cash from temporarily restricted sources, which is generally not available to meet current obligations, due to the restrictions. Thus, this ratio could overstate the organization's ability to meet its basic operating needs. For ratio purposes, the organization may want to exclude the restricted cash from this equation.

DAYS IN ACCOUNTS RECEIVABLE

Days in accounts receivable is a critical ratio, particularly in those nonprofits that provide client services. This ratio measures the average time that receivables are outstanding. This is also known as the average collection period. Higher ratio results lead to lower days cash on hand and potentially to greater short-term financing requirement. Management should always strive to keep this ratio as low as possible.

The days in accounts receivable ratio is expressed in the following equation:

$$\frac{\text{Net Accounts Receivable}}{\text{Net Service Revenues} / 365}$$

Thus, $9,200 / ($53,600 / 365) = 62.65 days in accounts receivable

AVERAGE AGE OF PLANT

This is a very important ratio for those nonprofit organizations that provide client/member services and have a policy of owning their fixed assets, particularly buildings and equipment. Average age of plant measures the average age in years of the organization's fixed assets. Values between 5.0 and 9.0 years will usually indicate a relatively young plant. In the case below, lower results indicate a younger plant, thereby typically enhancing client satisfaction, while higher results may indicate the opposite.

The average age of plant ratio is expressed in the following equation:

$$\frac{\text{Accumulated Depreciation}}{\text{Depreciation Expenses}}$$

Thus, $18,000 / $3,000 = 6.0 average age of plant

AVERAGE PAYMENT PERIOD

The average payment period ratio is the flip side of the days in accounts receivable. It measures the average time that elapses before the organization's current liabilities are paid. High values may indicate potential liquidity problems, particularly if there is a low level of days cash on hand.

The average payment period ratio is expressed in the following equation:

$$\frac{\text{Current Liabilities}}{(\text{Total Expenses} - \text{Depreciation}) / 365}$$

Thus, $7,500 / (($61,500 - $3,200) / 365) = 46.9 days average payment period

DEBT SERVICE COVERAGE

The debt service coverage ratio is one of the key debt ratios used by investment managers and bond rating agencies to determine the organization's ability to pay back its bond debt. It measures the relationship between the organization's bottom line cash and its annual debt service payments (principal + interest expense). A higher ratio, typically between 2.0 and 5.0, is preferred as it indicates a higher level of profitability compared to its debt obligations.

The debt service coverage ratio is expressed in the following equation:

$$\frac{\text{Excess of Support and Total Revenues over Expenses} + \text{Depreciation} + \text{Interest Expense}}{\text{Principal Payments} + \text{Interest Expense}}$$

Thus, ($6,400 + $3,000 + $3,200) / ($1,500 + $3,200) = 2.68 debt service coverage

RETURN ON NET ASSETS

This is a profitability ratio that is used to determine the organization's percentage return of total margin compared to its unrestricted net assets. The ratio measures the ability to fund additions and renovations without having to add new debt. The higher the result, the better.

The return on net assets ratio is expressed in the following equation:

$$\frac{\text{Excess of Support and Total Revenues over Expenses}}{\text{Unrestricted Net Assets}}$$

Thus, $6,400 / $32,600 = 19.6% return on net assets

OPERATING MARGIN PERCENTAGE

Operating margin percentage is one of the most popular ratios. It measures the organization's bottom line before non–operating revenues compared to its total revenues. The computed ratio allows the reader to quickly, and rather accurately, determine the extent of the organization's profitability on its core operations. Higher values are preferable.

The operating margin percentage ratio is expressed in the following equation:

$$\frac{\text{Excess of Support and Revenues over Expenses}}{\text{Total Support and Revenues}}$$

Thus, $5,200 / $66,700 = 7.8% operating margin

NET MARGIN PERCENTAGE

Like the operating margin percentage ratio, the net (or total) margin percentage ratio measures profitability of all revenues, including non–core returns. This typically means investment income, which is generally classified as non–operating and is reported below the operating margin (excess of operating revenues over expenses). Also, like the operating margin ratio, higher margins are preferred as a result.

The net margin percentage ratio is expressed in the following equation:

$$\frac{\text{Excess of Support and Total Revenues over Expenses}}{\text{Total Support and Revenues}}$$

Thus, $6,400 / $66,700 = 9.6% net margin

INTEREST EXPENSE PERCENTAGE

The board, or any other reader, may be interested in the rate being paid on its borrowed money. This interest expense percentage ratio measures the overall average interest rate being paid by the organization to finance its long-term debt. It allows the board to determine whether the ongoing rate is acceptable or whether refinancing should be explored.

The interest expense percentage ratio is expressed in the following equation:

$$\frac{\text{Total Interest Expense}}{\text{Current and Long-Term Bond Debt}}$$

Thus, \$3,200 / (\$1,500 + \$64,800) = 4.8% interest expense

INTEREST INCOME PERCENTAGE

The interest income percentage ratio is the flip side of the interest expense percentage. This ratio measures the overall average percentage earnings on all of the organization's assets with potential to invest. It allows the board to quickly understand the overall investment returns, which may in turn lead to altered decision making.

The interest income percentage ratio is expressed in the following equation:

$$\frac{\text{Total Interest Income + Dividend Income + Realized Gains on Securities}}{\text{Cash + Cash Equivalent + All Long-Term Investments}}$$

Thus, \$1,200 / (\$1,200 + \$6,500 + \$62,300 + \$10,000) = 1.35% interest income

There may be many other ratios that are important to the various nonprofit organizations. Boards need to decide any other metrics that they would like to see on a routine basis. The rule that should be employed for setting and monitoring metrics is whether the outcome of the metric has a critical, substantial impact on the organization's operations. The foregoing metrics are meant to be a starter set. The conversations that take place at the board and senior management levels to determine the appropriate metrics are worth all the time they take. It is an essential purpose of the board.

HINTS FOR BOARD MEMBERS

Make financial ratio analysis the first page of the monthly financial board review. Have it presented so that it is easy to determine any variance of these ratios between the set goal (budget) and the actual results.

Advanced Ways To Use Financial Information and Other Metrics To Gauge Organizational Performance: Balanced Scorecard

The foregoing financial ratios are extremely valuable to board members. If used appropriately and in a timely manner, they allow the board members to recognize a complete set of the organization's financial outcomes in a summarized fashion. When reported in a suitable format, they enhance the board's ability to move the organization along with improved decision making.

There is an additional management tool that will further allow the board to gain an even better understanding of the organization's operations as a whole — the balanced scorecard. Balanced scorecards have gained acceptance over the past decade for their ability to paint a relatively complete picture of organizational performance. Scorecards take into account the key financial elements, as previously reported in this book, as well as the other key elements that drive the outcomes mandated by the board.

It should be noted that the upcoming discussion on the balanced scorecard may appear to be applicable only to larger nonprofit organizations, or those nonprofits that have competitors, both for-profit and nonprofit. But, that is not the case. As you read this section, keep in mind the mission and the various goals your organization has committed to fulfill. Each of the goals should fit into one of the balanced scorecard quadrants for review. The scorecard is simply a means by which the organization can keep track of its outcomes as compared to its goals.

"The balanced scorecard provides executives with a comprehensive framework that translates a company's vision and strategy into a coherent set of performance measures," note Kaplan and Norton. (*The Balanced Scorecard*, Kaplan and Norton, Harvard Business School Press, 1996, page 24)

This tool extends beyond the traditional mission and vision statements to communicate a more specific set of requirements to the various stakeholders in an enterprise. Furthermore, "the balanced scorecard retains financial measurement as a critical summary of managerial and business performance, but it highlights a more general and integrated set of measurements that link customer, internal process, employee, and system performance to long-term financial success." (Kaplan and Norton, page 21)

In short, the balanced scorecard utilizes four different quadrants of performance measures to create a natural and continuous feedback loop (which can then be used to monitor and improve the organization's level of effectiveness). The suggested four quadrants are

- Financial Perspective

- Customer Perspective

- Internal Perspective

- Learning and Growth

An organization may use different performance measures within these four groupings. Box 7 lists some of the more common line items that are utilized in the balanced scorecard. Once again, it is important to keep in mind that each organization must use those items that represent its own particular critical success factors.

BOX 7
BALANCED SCORECARD QUADRANTS

Financial Perspective

- Return on Capital

- Competitive Position

- Volume Growth

- Reduced Cash Outlays

- Improved Cash Receipts

Customer Perspective

- Stakeholder Satisfaction

Internal Perspective

- Product Innovation

- Perfect Orders (reduce errors)

Learning and Growth

- Strategic Awareness

- Mandated Hours of Education per Employee

HOW TO DEVELOP THE SCORECARD

There are a number of ways to develop a balanced scorecard. These methods include

- *Developing an executable organizational business strategy* — What are the important elements that will make the business successful?

- *Describing the strategy* — This helps users and performers understand the reasons behind the strategy, allowing for much greater buy-in.

- *Designing and developing the scorecard framework with strategic objectives and performance measurements* — These performance measures should closely follow the strategic objectives outlined by the organization.

Thus, the scorecard does not stand alone as an unrelated set of metrics. Instead, it is the financial and nonfinancial goals setting and monitoring the system for the organization's preferred outcomes.

BALANCED SCORECARD IN NONPROFIT ORGANIZATIONS

All nonprofit organizations, regardless of the industry they represent, can benefit from utilization of the balanced scorecard. Exhibit 8 illustrates some of the specific elements that could and should be used in the measure of performance, let's say, for a nonprofit hospital.

EXHIBIT 8   **HEALTHCARE INSIGHTS**

BRILLIANT HOSPITAL BALANCED SCORECARD

Financial Perspective	2.19	Needs Improvement *
Return on Net Assets	3.60	Good
Competitive Position	.83	Unsatisfactory
Volume Growth	1.00	Poor
Reduced Cash Outlays	3.50	Excellent
Improved Cash Receipts	2.00	Needs Improvement
Customer Perspective	2.20	Needs Improvement
Patient Satisfaction	2.20	Needs Improvement
Internal Perspective	3.31	Good
Product Innovation	3.00	Good
Perfect Orders (reduce errors)	2.50	Needs Improvement
Quality Indicators	4.00	Excellent
Clinical Outcomes	3.75	Good
Learning and Growth	3.00	Good
Strategic Awareness	3.00	Good
Leadership Surveys	3.20	Good
Mandated Education Hours per Employee	2.80	Needs Improvement

Brilliant Overall Performance	**Score**	**Weight**	**Weighted Score**
Financial Perspective	2.19	25.0%	0.55
Customer Perspective	2.20	25.0%	0.55
Internal Perspective	3.31	25.0%	0.83
Learning and Growth	3.00	25.0%	0.75
Total Score		2.67	Needs Improvement

* 0 = Poor = lowest 10th percentile of the benchmark
1 = Unsatisfactory = 11th – 25th percentile of the benchmark
2 = Needs Improvement = 25th – 50th percentile of the benchmark
3 = Good = 50th – 75th percentile of the benchmark
4 = Very Good = 75th – 90th percentile of the benchmark
5 = Excellent = 90th – 100th percentile of the benchmark

Source: TRAC decisions support management accountability software
www.healthcareinsightsllc.com

As you can see, this list goes well beyond the financial indicators, which allow users to gain a more complete insight into the goals and achievements of the organization. These are all highly critical outcomes for this nonprofit hospital and it is crucial that the hospital sets its goals around all of them, not just financial outcomes. In fact, excelling in the nonfinancial elements is likely to bring greater financial success than downplaying the nonfinancial elements.

Further, it is important to look outside your own organization in setting the goals and then monitoring the results for the scorecard. In Exhibit 9 (on page 46), the individual indicators of the financial quadrants are analyzed against the organizations' own goals and against their peers, as represented in the last column by a proprietary benchmark service. It is extremely important to be aware of how your own organization is performing relative to its peers, since business is likely to be gained or lost, based on the results.

BALANCING THE SCORECARD

So far, it is clear that the scorecard is valuable in helping to set organizational goals and monitor their outcomes. It is important to recognize that not all metrics are equal. Some are more valuable to the organization's ultimate result than others. Thus it is important to value these metrics and develop a weighting mechanism around the major categories. In this way, we will be able to "balance" the scorecard according to the metric's values.

A balanced scorecard will generally have a relative consistency around the four quadrants, with no one quadrant having a disproportionate share of the total allocated to it. For example, an unbalanced scorecard might allocate 70 percent of the total to the financial quadrant, leaving only 30 percent for the other three quadrants. While this type of allocation may have a short-term benefit, in the long term it could have a deleterious impact on the organization's outcomes, financial and nonfinancial. A balanced approach could be 30 percent each to financial and internal process and 20 percent each to customer perspective and learning and growth. It is through the balancing of the scorecard that the organization can determine and value its most important success criteria in an objective manner.

As you can see, the balanced scorecard is an excellent, available technique that should be used by nonprofit organizations to accelerate excellence in management and provide the best opportunity for the organization to achieve its stated goals.

EXHIBIT 9   HEALTHCARE INSIGHTS

FINANCIAL INDICATORS
BALANCED SCORECARD DRILLDOWN

Indicator	Positive Trend	FY 2000	Budget 2001	Sept 2001	YTD 2001	Comparison to Benchmark
Financial Profitability						
Operating Margin	Up	0.05	0.04	0.04	0.05	Very Good
Total Margin	Up	0.08	0.07	0.11	0.13	Excellent
EBIDA Revenue	Up	0.18	0.16	0.17	0.16	Good
EBIDA Assets	Up	0.08	0.07	0.10	0.11	Good
Return on Equity	Up	0.10	0.07	0.09	0.08	Good
Liquidity						
Current	Up	0.01	0.01	0.01	0.01	Poor
Days in Patient Accounts Receivable	Down	82.00	91.00	85.00	86.00	Poor
Average Payment Period	Down	140.00	152.00	143.00	148.00	Unsatisfactory
Capital Structure						
Equity Financing	Up	0.15	0.14	0.15	0.14	Poor
Long-Term Debt to Capitalization	Down	0.72	0.72	0.71	0.72	Unsatisfactory
Cash Flow to Total Debt	Up	0.04	0.03	0.04	-0.03	Poor
Annual Debt Service Coverage	Up	0.06	0.07	0.07	0.01	Poor
Maximum Debt Service Coverage	Up	0.06	0.07	0.07	0.01	Poor
Cushion	Up	0.01	0.01	0.01	0.00	Poor
Asset Efficiency						
Total Asset Turnover	Up	1.28	1.18	1.26	1.25	Very Good
Inventory	Up	74.00	70.00	66.00	65.00	Good

Source: TRAC decisions support management accountability software
www.healthcareinsightsllc.com

Additional Management Techniques

In the preceding sections, there has been a lot of discussion about utilizing financial information to determine organizational performance through ratio analysis and the balanced scorecard. Both of these techniques are essential to the proper analysis and understanding of the organization's performance. There are additional management techniques that should be used in conjunction with ratio analysis and the balanced scorecard to further enhance this understanding. These techniques take the established analysis and provide additional information to the reader, placing the results in context.

Trending

The first of these additional management techniques is the use of trend information across time. Without trending, the reader may only have the actual and budgeted values in which to build an organizational perspective. The use of trending greatly enhances the understanding of the direction that the organization is heading.

Take as an example one of the financial values that was previously identified, days cash on hand, all sources. Given the information already reported in the financial statements, and assuming that the organization reported a page of ratio analysis, the reader would know that the 2002 days cash on hand, all sources was 499.15 days, while the 2001 result was 489.72. Perhaps no additional information would be required because the result is clearly excellent. But, that is not necessarily the whole story. Exhibit 10 shows the trend of days cash on hand for the prior five years. Additionally, the chart contains a *narrative explanation* for the substantial increase in cash in 1999. Boards, and other readers, obtain important information from well-put-together trend graphs, charts, and tables. They should be used routinely to provide the essential elements of organizational performance.

Exhibit 10

Days Cash on Hand, All Sources
Five-Year Trend
For the Years Ended December 31, 1998 – 2002

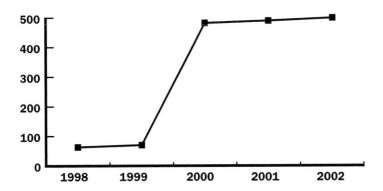

This chart shows steadily increasing cash in the organization. A substantial increase occurred in 2000, when the organization borrowed $58.0 million in order to finance certain fixed asset needs and to create cash reserves. Positive operating results have allowed the cash to continue to increase.

BENCHMARKING

Benchmarking is another essential management technique. It allows the organization to compare its outcomes, financial and nonfinancial, with its peers. Without benchmarking comparisons, the organization will not be able to determine whether it is operating at the best possible level of performance. We have already reviewed some benchmarking issues while looking at balanced scorecard concepts.

Let's take a further look at benchmarking with the following debt service coverage example. Debt service coverage is designed to measure the relationship between the organization's bottom line cash and its annual debt service payments (principal + interest expense). This indicates the organization's ability to pay back its bonds.

Without the benchmarking information, the reader would only know the following results — debt service coverage for 2002 was 2.68 and for 2001 it was 2.32. Further, we have been advised that a higher value is preferable. But, we do not know an average (possibly median) value across a group of organizations that perform similar functions as our organization. Perhaps we have even been given trend information, such as in Exhibit 11. This chart shows a significant decline in the debt service coverage ratio and a reduced ability to borrow additional funds in the near future.

EXHIBIT 11

**Debt Service Coverage
Five-Year Trend
For the Years Ended December 31, 1998 – 2002**

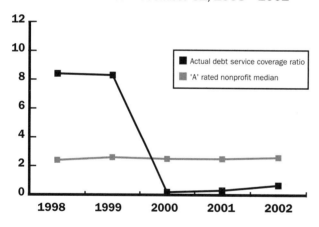

This chart shows a substantial decrease in debt service coverage occurred in 2000, when the organization borrowed $58.0 million. This increased the prior outstanding debt balance from $10.0 million to $68.0 million. Subsequently, the organization had a lower debt service coverage ratio. This indicates that the organization has less opportunity to finance additional borrowings in the near future, particularly since its ratio is considerably lower than the benchmark median for similar 'A' rated nonprofit organizations.

Still, without the benchmarking ratio results reported on the graph, we would not know what ratio would be considered acceptable to a bond-rating agency in order to obtain a rating of "A" or better. To obtain this information, we need to look for benchmarking results from those nonprofit organizations that have already borrowed funds. By gathering the information on these ratios for similar types of organizations, a median result can be obtained to alert the reader to variances. Let's say that the benchmark median for debt service coverage in 2002 is 4.6. This allows the reader, and particularly the board, to determine the value that this organization needs to strive for. Assuming that benchmarking values exist for your type of organization, it becomes another essential element of understanding financial statements.

HINTS FOR BOARD MEMBERS

Develop a balanced scorecard set of goals and use it as the first page of the monthly report to the board. The balanced scorecard will represent all of the vital operational elements, including financial, that were previously approved by the board, and the comparison of these goals with actual results. Thus, the balanced scorecard provides the best summary of compliance/noncompliance with the board's approved financial and nonfinancial goals.

Conclusion

To many board members, it may seem that the amount of information they are required to know is overwhelming. There is the mission to consider, the operations to comprehend, the customer/client/member satisfaction to contemplate, and the finances to grasp. True, this can seem a daunting task, but gaining an understanding of the issues covered in this book gets you off to a very good start.

Nonprofit board members must actively participate in the dialogues and discussions that take place both in the finance committee and in the full board meeting. They must use their own good judgment and experience to speak up and express opinions on financial subjects that will impact the organization. If an item is not explained to the members' satisfaction, clarification should be sought. If it appears too complex, make sure that management simplifies the item so that it can be understood. If it does not seem to meet any of the generally accepted accounting principles highlighted in the book, question it.

It is the board's role and responsibility to serve as the watchdog over management's operations. It is the board's role and responsibility to ensure that the mission is met. It is the board's role and responsibility to substantiate that the financial requirements of the organization have been properly set and met. These are serious roles and responsibilities.

Understanding nonprofit financial statements is the basic building block. Use it!

Appendix

SUPPLEMENTAL AUDITOR REPORTS

The nonprofit board should be aware that there are two other reports that may be included in the auditor's annual report. These reports are intended to provide additional information to board members, allowing for the greater understanding of their management's performance under accounting principles and practices. Additional information about these reports, (1) SAS 61 letter, and (2) Reports Required in Accordance with Office of Management and Budget Circular A-133, follow. Additionally, other supplemental information may also be requested.

SAS 61 LETTER

The American Institute of Certified Public Accountants has issued the Statement on Auditing Standards No. 61 (SAS 61) — Communication with Audit Committees. This standard-setting body requires communication of various matters to the audit committee, or its equivalent, on an annual basis. This report is intended solely for the use of the board of directors and management.

The communications required as per SAS 61 include the following:

The Auditor's Responsibility under Auditing Standards Generally Accepted in the United States of America
The auditor should communicate the level of responsibility assumed for the internal control structure, illegal acts, and other matters under generally accepted auditing standards.

Significant Accounting Policies and Unusual Transactions
The auditor should determine that the board is informed about the initial selection of, and changes in, significant accounting policies as well as the methods used to account for significant unusual transactions.

Management Judgments and Accounting Estimates
The board should be informed about the process used by management in forming particularly sensitive accounting estimates and about the basis for the auditor's conclusions regarding the reasonableness of those estimates.

Audit Adjustments
All proposed adjustments arising from the audit should be communicated to the board.

Disagreements with Management
Disagreements with management, whether or not satisfactorily resolved, about matters that could be significant to the entity's financial statements or the auditor's report, should be communicated to the board.

Consultation with Other Accountants

When the auditor is aware that management has consulted with other accountants about significant accounting or auditing matters, the auditor's views about the subject of the consultation should be communicated to the board.

Major Issues Discussed with Management Prior to Retention

Any major issues that were discussed with management in connection with initial or recurring retention should be communicated to the board.

Difficulties Encountered in Performing the Audit

Serious difficulties encountered in dealing with management that relate to the performance of the audit are required to be brought to the attention of the board.

Reportable Conditions and Material Weaknesses Letter

Any reportable conditions (or significant deficiencies in the design or structure of the internal control structure) coming to the auditor's attention during the audit should be communicated to the board.

The auditors are required to report any reportable conditions and material weaknesses noted during the audit to the audit committee or its equivalent (finance committee or board of directors).

Reportable conditions involve matters relating to significant deficiencies in the design or operation of the internal control structure that could adversely affect the organization's ability to record, process, summarize, and report financial data consistent with the assertions of management in the financial statements.

A *material weakness* is a reportable condition in which the design or operation of one or more of the internal control structure elements does not reduce to a relatively low level; the risk that errors or irregularities in amounts that would be material in relation to the financial statements being audited may occur and not be detected within a timely period by employees in the normal course of performing their assigned functions.

HINTS FOR BOARD MEMBERS

Boards should be sure to obtain this SAS 61 management letter during the auditor's annual presentation to the board. Most importantly, make sure that management has provided action plans to correct any of the issues addressed. These action plans should be included in the auditor's report and must include timetables for completions. Finally, the board should schedule specific agenda items throughout the upcoming year to review the level of completion to each item originally presented in the SAS 61 management letter.

REPORTS REQUIRED IN ACCORDANCE WITH OFFICE OF MANAGEMENT AND BUDGET CIRCULAR A-133

If the organization receives federal funding over a certain threshold, it may be subject to an Office of Management and Budget (OMB) audit. This type of audit requires additional reporting as part of the reports (see below) to the audit committee or its equivalent.

- Independent Auditor's Report on Compliance and on Internal Control over Financial Reporting Based on an Audit of Financial Statements Performed in Accordance with Government Auditing Standards

- Independent Auditor's Report on Compliance with Requirements Applicable to Each Major Program and Internal Control over Compliance in Accordance with OMB Circular A-133

- Schedule of Expenditures of Federal Awards

- Notes to Schedule of Expenditures of Federal Awards

- Schedule of Findings and Questioned Costs

OTHER SUPPLEMENTAL INFORMATION

Management, the audit committee, or its equivalent may request that other information or reports are included as part of the reports issued by the auditors. The supplemental information or reports are presented for purposes of additional analysis and are not a required part of the basic financial statements. Such information is often subject to the auditing procedures applied in the audit of the basic financial statements and the auditors will often state their opinion as to whether this information is fairly stated in all material respects in relation to the basic financial statements taken as a whole.

A good example of some supplemental reports and information include

- Consolidating statements

- Investment statistics

- Grant and contract summaries

SUGGESTED RESOURCES

Andringa, Robert C. *Nonprofit Board Answer Book II: Beyond the Basics.* Washington, DC: BoardSource, 2002.
Learn how to answer the hard questions posed by seasoned nonprofit executives who have moved beyond the basics of nonprofit management to confront the tougher issues. Building on the success of the *Nonprofit Board Answer Book,* this collection of questions and answers explores the governance successes of nonprofit organizations, details action steps, and provides the facts you need to move into such uncharted waters as launching a for-profit subsidiary, re-branding your organization, or surviving a merger. You'll learn how to effectively deal with thorny risk management, conflict of interest, and performance issues.

Fry, Robert P. *Creating and Using Investment Policies: A Guide for Nonprofit Boards.* Washington, DC: BoardSource, 1997.
As the financial conditions of a nonprofit improve and a reserve fund becomes a reality, the board members have the difficult task of deciding how to best manage and invest the funds. This booklet answers many of the questions concerning the basics of investing, the legal basis for investment theory, cash management issues, necessity for an investment advisor, and the appropriate board member involvement in investment management.

Lang, Andrew S. *Financial Responsibilities of Nonprofit Boards.* Washington, DC: BoardSource, 2003.
Provide your board members with an understanding of their financial responsibilities including an overview of financial oversight and ways to ensure against risk. Written in non-technical language, this booklet will help your board understand financial planning, the IRS Form 990, and the audit process. Also included are financial board and staff job descriptions and charts on all the financial documents and reports, including due dates and filing procedures.

McLaughlin, Thomas. *Presenting: Nonprofit Financials.* Washington, DC: BoardSource, 2001.
Presenting: Nonprofit Financials is a ready-made on-screen presentation that can be used as a traditional graphics presentation, as overhead transparency slides, or printed out for handouts. Each slide is accompanied by a set of presentation notes and talking points to guide the discussion. Also included is a 12-page user's guide with suggestions for training board members on their financial responsibilities, instructions for using the presentation, and tips for providing proper fiduciary oversight.

Sorrells, Michael, and Andrew S. Lang. *The IRS Form 990: A Window Into Nonprofits.* Washington, DC: BoardSource, 2001.
This booklet describes the Form 990 and its purposes, and includes a step-by-step guide through each part of the form. Also included is a discussion of the filing requirements and disclosure rules. The authors point to sensitive areas that the board should pay particular attention to before submitting.

About the Author

Steven Berger is President of Healthcare Insights, LLC, which specializes in the teaching and consulting of health care financial management issues. Healthcare Insights has also produced and sells TRAC, a decision support management accountability software system. Prior to his role at Healthcare Insights, LLC, Mr. Berger was Vice President, Finance for seven years at a 250-bed Highland Park Hospital in suburban Chicago, Illinois. Before Highland Park Hospital and since 1978, he has been a hospital/health system finance officer in New York, New Jersey, and Missouri.

Mr. Berger has many years of health care financial management experience. He holds a Bachelor of Science degree in history and a Masters in Science degree in accounting from the State University of New York at Binghamton. He is a CPA, and a Fellow of the Healthcare Financial Management Association where he recently served as president of the First Illinois Chapter. Mr. Berger is also a Diplomate of the American College of Healthcare Executives. He has presented many health care finance-related seminars throughout the United States and Canada, including three two-day classes: Fundamentals of Healthcare Financial Management, Turning Data into Useful Information, and Hospital Financial Management for the Nonfinancial Manager. He has also presented board-level financial training for BoardSource at its annual meeting.

Mr. Berger has written several articles on health care financial and general management issues that were published in *Healthcare Financial Management* magazine, including an April 2002 column on management accountability. He is the author of two hospital/health care financial management books. *Fundamentals of Healthcare Financial Management*, first published in 1999 by McGraw-Hill and the Healthcare Financial Management Association, was written from a practitioner's point of view and is a distillation of Mr. Berger's many years on the inside of health care institutions. The second edition of the book was published by Jossey-Bass in January 2002. Additionally, Mr. Berger is the co-author of HFMA's *Introduction to Hospital Accounting, 4th Edition*, which was published in the summer of 2002 by Kendall Hunt.

Finally, Mr. Berger has recently completed a term as president of the Board of Turning Point, a 501(c)(3) nonprofit community mental health agency. It is this experience that led to the creation of this book.

Additional information on training, consulting, or management accountability software (operating and capital budgeting, position control, balanced scorecard, labor productivity, monitoring and measuring goals through automated e-mail alerts) can be obtained at www.healthcareinsightsllc.com or e-mail at sberger@healthcareinsightsllc.com.